Original title:
Life, Laughter, and Lemons

Copyright © 2025 Creative Arts Management OÜ
All rights reserved.

Author: Isabella Rosemont
ISBN HARDBACK: 978-1-80566-097-2
ISBN PAPERBACK: 978-1-80566-392-8

A Dance of Distinction

In the kitchen, pots collide,
Spoons are twirling, side to side.
A recipe gone wildly wrong,
Yet laughter echoes, like a song.

The cat leaps high, a graceful sway,
Napping chefs, in disarray.
Flour clouds paint the walls with glee,
What a mess, but oh, what glee!

Savoring the Wild Journey

A road trip through the twists and bends,
With songs from past, and snacks to send.
Maps are useless, directions stray,
But giggles guide us, come what may.

Each pit stop's like a carnival,
The ice cream melting, a free-for-all.
With every bump and silly shout,
The sweetest memories come about.

Dancing with Sunshine

The sun peeks in, a playful tease,
Morning hair and mismatched keys.
Coffee spills, a comic sight,
Yet morning grins make it all right.

Outside, the breeze does cha-cha moves,
With sideward glances, and funny grooves.
A game of tag with shadows cast,
In silly moments, we find our blast.

The Sparkle in the Ordinary

A to-do list turned into a jest,
Juggling chores, we do our best.
Lost the socks? Just wear them bright,
In mismatched fashion, we'll delight.

The mundane shines with vibrant flair,
Chasing bubbles through the air.
In simple things, we find our bliss,
Who knew the mundane could feel like this?

Lively Days and Zesty Nights

In the morning, joy takes flight,
Dancing shadows greet the light.
Silly hats and cheerful tunes,
Spin around like funny loons.

Evening brings a playful tease,
Jokes exchanged like summer breeze.
Twinkling stars wink at our plight,
As we giggle into the night.

Embracing the Unexpected

Surprises pop like bubble wraps,
Every fumble leads to laps.
Tiptoeing on unexpected grind,
We lose our worries, leave them behind.

A sudden splash, a funny slip,
Moments shared on laughter's trip.
Embrace the turns that life may take,
Build memories, no chance to break.

A Slice of Sunshine

Sunshine served with a sprinkle of glee,
A smoothie mix, just sip and see.
Wobbly chairs and funny spills,
Tickled fancy, laughter fills.

Sitting by the window's light,
Silly stories come to bite.
A slice of joy on a plate revealed,
With every giggle, our hearts healed.

Radiant Reverie

In dreams we chase the brightest hues,
Whimsy dances, a playful muse.
Chasing clouds, we take a ride,
Giggling shadows, side by side.

Each moment whispers, 'Join the fun!',
Painting rainbows, on the run.
With open hearts, we'll find the way,
To sparkle brightly, come what may.

Mirthful Misadventures

In the garden of mishaps, we stumble and trip,
Chasing after the giggles, letting joy slip.
Fruits of our folly hang low on the vine,
Squeeze out the sweetness, make the sour shine.

A jester in overalls, antics on display,
Pulled a face at the fair; the crowd's in dismay.
With cada roar of laughter, my shoes get a splash,
In puddles of whimsy, we dance, twist, and clash.

Lemonade rivers flow where the wild critters roam,
Sipping on sunshine, we build our small home.
Each hiccup a giggle, each misstep a cheer,
As we paint the dull moments with colors sincere.

Mirth swirls around us like butterflies bright,
Fluttering softly, they tease us to flight.
In a whirl of confusion, we spring and we sway,
Finding joy in the chaos, come dance out and play.

Rhapsody of the Orchard

In an orchard where chuckles grow sweeter than dreams,
A squirrel stole my sandwich; or so it seems.
With a hop and a skip, he danced on the grass,
Leaving me with a banana, a colorful farce.

A picnic of blunders lays spread on the ground,
Laughter erupts with each clatter and sound.
We toss away worries, like crumbs to the breeze,
In a symphony of smiles, we gather with ease.

The wind has a giggle, as apples take flight,
A poetic disaster, a comical sight.
With mischief a-plenty, the sun's glowing bright,
We sip on the moments, with all of our might.

As shadows grow longer, the twilight descends,
In a rhapsody playful, where joy never ends.
With each silly story, our hearts intertwine,
In the orchard of laughter, together we shine.

Quenching Life's Thirst

A zesty splash on a sunny day,
Sour smiles chase the frowns away.
Bottled giggles, a twist of fate,
Sip it slowly, this drink of state.

Frothy laughter in a bubbling cup,
Mistakes are just hiccups, so lift it up.
With every sip, the world feels bright,
Pucker your lips, hold on tight!

Infused with Brilliance

A swirl of zest in a blender's song,
Funny faces where we all belong.
Chortles rolling like a citrus breeze,
Mix it up, shake off the freeze!

Jests so sour, they bring forth cheer,
In every punchline, we find our gear.
Bright and bubbly, we dance with glee,
Can't take a drink without spilling tea!

Brightening the Mundane

Turn a gray day into a punchy twist,
With every giggle, can't resist.
Squeeze that joy into every space,
Wear that grin, transform the place!

Hiccups of laughter, bright confetti,
Moments shared, always ready and petty.
Mix up the mundane with a splash of cheer,
Every sour note makes the sweet more clear!

Sprightly Chronicles

In tales where sunlight meets desire,
Lemon tales spark a whimsical fire.
Each smile's a slice, juiced from a grin,
Gather round, let the fun begin!

Whirling stories with zesty flair,
Sipping on joy, we haven't a care.
Every hiccup turns into song,
In these chronicles, we all belong!

Sweetness in the Squeeze

In a world of yellow roundness, glows,
Juicy bursts from the highs and the lows.
When things get sour, don't you fret,
A twist of fate's what you can get.

Giggles bubbling up, oh so bright,
Mirth in every ounce, a sheer delight.
Squeeze the moments, let joy unfold,
A zesty tale that's yet to be told.

Gritty Moments and Golden Rays

Underneath the sun's warm embrace,
Unexpected slips put smiles on our face.
When storms arrive, we bravely stand,
Sipper of sunshine, life's own brand.

A squirt of humor, sharp yet sweet,
In every wrong turn, a chance to meet.
Golden rays that dance through the gloom,
Turning grits into zest, ah, how they bloom.

Whimsical Whirls of Citrus Bliss

Round and round on a merry-go-craze,
Zesty spins that set hearts ablaze.
With pulpy tales and good times ahead,
We laugh 'til our worries are all but dead.

In every swirl, a chuckle arises,
Juicy fun in endless surprises.
Citrussy chuckles, we gather in cheer,
To embrace every moment we hold dear.

A Slice of Glee and Grit

Chop it up, share a piece of this fun,
Zesty giggles for everyone.
In the kitchen chaos, we gather near,
With sweet little stories and some light cheer.

When days get tough, let's toss in some zest,
A sprinkle of joy put to the test.
With every slice, we carve out delight,
Gritty and sweet, we dance through the night.

Grins and Grapefruits

In the sun, we dance with joy,
Twist and turn like a playful toy.
Lemonade dreams in a frothy glass,
Giggling warm as the moments pass.

With zesty smiles, we share the fun,
Juggling fruits, we laugh and run.
Every ripe slice, a silly cheer,
Bubbling bright without a care here.

Juicy Memories Beneath the Sky

Under clouds of fluffy fluff,
We toss and catch the citrus stuff.
Giggles echo in summer's glow,
Memories sprout where the laughter flows.

A mischief brew of yellow hue,
Sipping sunshine, we make it new.
With every squeeze, we spill the glee,
Bright moments burst in jubilee.

Orchard of Delight

In a grove where chuckles bloom,
Joyful sounds chase away all gloom.
Swinging high from a branch so spry,
With every leap, we reach the sky.

Fruitful laughter fills the air,
Tickled hearts, without a care.
A harvest rich in play and fun,
Every giggle beneath the sun.

The Playfulness of Being

In the park, we hop and play,
Chasing shadows of the day.
With every giggle, we take a chance,
Twisting thoughts in a silly dance.

A splash of color, a burst of sound,
Joyful echoes all around.
In our hearts, the warmth ignites,
Savoring silly, carefree flights.

Whimsy in Every Drop

In a world where giggles bloom,
Silly moments fill the room.
A sip of joy flows from a cup,
And troubles seem to shrink, to sup.

The sky wears smiles, clouds dance around,
Every puddle hides laughter found.
With every splash and every cheer,
The playful spirit draws us near.

Sun-Kissed Adventures

Bright days lead us down the lane,
Where every moment's free from strain.
The sun's warm glow, a playful tease,
Brings forth the fun with every breeze.

We chase the shadows, we run like fools,
Splashing through ripples, breaking rules.
With friends beside and smiles so wide,
We find our joy in every stride.

Notes of Contrast

A sweet surprise within a tart,
Contradictions dance within the heart.
From joyful highs to silly lows,
Each twist and turn, the laughter grows.

With every sour bite we find,
A sparkle sweet, a twist designed.
Life's melodies, both sharp and sweet,
Compose a tune that's hard to beat.

The Juggle of Sour and Sweet

Twirling jests in circus glee,
Balancing joys, just wait and see.
The sour face soon turns to grin,
As laughter bubbles up within.

Walking tightropes, hearts in flight,
We share our dreams in morning light.
Through juggling acts of fun and cheer,
We catch the moments, hold them dear.

Chasing the Golden Horizon

On the edge of the world where the sun plays,
Chasing dreams in the light of its rays.
With a skip and a hop, we twirl around,
Collecting bright wishes that leap and bound.

With friends in tow, we dance through the day,
In a quirky parade, we laugh and sway.
The horizon beckons, oh, what a sight,
With giggles and grins, everything feels right.

Sunlit Smiles

In the warmth of the glow, joy finds its way,
Tickling our hearts in a whimsical play.
We juggle our troubles, tossing them high,
As the warmth wraps us close, like a sweet goodbye.

A splash of the sun and a sprinkle of cheer,
Every step we take, we shed all our fear.
With a wink and a nod, joy fills the air,
In silly antics, we find treasures rare.

The Art of Savoring

With a pinch of whimsy and a laugh or two,
We savor each moment, fresh as the dew.
A stumble, a giggle, we dance in a jest,
Each second a morsel, oh, what a fest!

We paint the world bright with our playful strokes,
Creating memories wrapped in pure jokes.
With the sparkle of mischief in every bite,
Life's greatest delights shine dazzlingly bright.

Golden Sips of Happiness

Pour a cup of cheer, let the fun overflow,
Every drop a delight in the sun's warm glow.
With silly straws twisted, we sip with glee,
Every chuckle a toast, just you and me.

We gather our giggles and roll them like dice,
Spinning tales of joy, oh, isn't it nice?
With each golden sip, we banish the gloom,
In this playful dance, we create our own room.

The Flavor of Hope

In a kitchen, pots collide,
A twist of fate, a zesty ride.
Squeezed and squeezed, a bright delight,
Turning sour into pure sunlight.

Giggles rise with every slice,
A sprinkle here, a dash of spice.
The world transforms, a citrus cheer,
As sunny flavors draw us near.

We'll dance around, a fruity spree,
With every taste, we feel so free.
A drop of sunshine on our tongues,
In every note, a song is sung.

So grab a cup, let laughter flow,
With bright concoctions, let it glow.
This potion makes the spirits lift,
A spark of joy, our double gift.

Shimmering Citrus Dreams

Underneath the starry glare,
We sip a drink, float on air.
Bubbles pop and laughter rings,
In every sip, a fairy sings.

Fruitful visions in the night,
With every twist, the world feels right.
Citrus kisses in the breeze,
A zany dance that makes us squeeze.

Jokes and jests in every glass,
We swirl the night as moments pass.
Bright-colored drinks bring smiles anew,
A citrus wish, a dream come true.

So join the fun, let worries fade,
With every laugh, new plans are made.
In shimmering dreams, we find our way,
Where sunshine colors every day.

Zesty Inspirations

In a garden where colors grow,
A sprinkle of zest will steal the show.
Sunshine smiles from every vine,
Creating scenes that feel divine.

Slicing fruits with joyful glee,
Each piece reveals a mystery.
Mixing flavors, bold and bright,
Painting treasures in the light.

A burst of joy, a playful spark,
As laughter dances in the dark.
Share a taste, discover new heights,
With zesty jokes and sweet delights.

So let the flavors form a bond,
With every sip, we go beyond.
In spicy tales, our hearts unite,
With every laugh, everything feels right.

Serene Shadows and Bright Lights

In the twilight, shadows play,
While stars begin to light the way.
A sprinkle of fun, an evening cheer,
As laughter echoes, bright and clear.

Citrus sunbeams, in full bloom,
Banishing any trace of gloom.
With every joke, the night ignites,
In gentle whispers, joyful sights.

Creativity flows with ease,
As flavors mix like summer breeze.
In the quiet, we find delight,
Wrapped in dreams, our hearts take flight.

So raise a glass to moments shared,
Where every twist brings joy declared.
In shadows bright and laughter's song,
We find a world where we belong.

The Sound of Citrus Laughter

In a grove where sunshine plays,
Bright fruits swing in merry ways.
A jabber of joy dances around,
While zestful giggles echo the ground.

With each squeeze, a grin appears,
Chasing shadows, banishing fears.
Peeled and pouted, the whole fruit's glee,
Spills like sunshine for all to see.

Lively Moments Under the Lemon Tree

Beneath the branches, time takes flight,
Chasing giggles, warm and bright.
Friends gather round with playful cheer,
A feast of joy that's oh so near.

With zesty talk and playful sips,
We toast the day with cheerful quips.
Every bright spark, a tale to share,
In this moment, without a care.

Bright Juices of the Heart

Squeezed delights in every cup,
Swirling laughter, never stop!
Each droplet dances, a merry song,
As we sip and smile all day long.

Sticky fingers, a playful mess,
With every drop, we feel so blessed.
Sunshine smiles and winks galore,
Our cheerful spirits forever soar.

Playful Rhymes in Golden Light

In a garden where joy unfolds,
Chasing dreams, as the story's told.
Sprouting jests beneath the sun,
With every giggle, life's more fun.

Golden rays weave through the trees,
Tickling souls like a gentle breeze.
We dance on air with every twist,
For in this moment, we can't resist.

Zestful Journeys

In a land where sunbeams dance,
Where giggles chase a chance,
Orange peels scatter wide,
And joy is a joyful ride.

Straw hats and silly shoes,
Lemons bring vibrant hues,
With each twist and every turn,
A zest for fun we earn.

Sour faces turn to grins,
As we spin and toss and spin,
Adventure calls with a laugh,
In this hilarious path.

Bubbles rise in the air,
Hiccups, giggles, everywhere,
With a wink and a waddle,
We wobble and we twaddle.

A Toast to Brightness

Raise your glasses, toast the cheer,
With sparkling drinks, we persevere,
A twist of fun in every sip,
A burst of joy in each tiny trip.

Slice the fruit, watch it gleam,
Sunshine captured in a dream,
Riding waves of laughter's tide,
Whirl around in citrus pride.

Silly faces, vibrant hats,
Life's too short for somber chats,
With every chuckle, let it grow,
The brighter path, the more we glow.

So sip away, let giggles play,
In the bright and zesty fray,
Toast to moments, funny and sweet,
With citrus joy, we feel complete.

Cheery Citrus Symphony

In orchards where the laughter sings,
Golden rays and silly flings,
A symphony of bright delight,
Tunes of joy take sudden flight.

Juicy notes in every laugh,
Squeezed tight in a happy half,
We dance beneath the warming sun,
Each hearty chuckle, a little fun.

Lemonade rivers flow with glee,
Waves of mirth, come join me!
Catch the rhythm, sway with flair,
In the sweet and zesty air.

Playful sounds echo all around,
In this citrus symphony found,
With every burst of playful zest,
We find our hearts are truly blessed.

The Essence of Sweetness

In the garden, bright and bold,
Stories of joy unfold,
With every grin and silly joke,
A sprinkle of fun in every poke.

Peeling laughter, fresh and bright,
Chasing shadows out of sight,
The essence of joy, pure and fine,
Captured in sweet, sunlit wine.

A wink, a giggle, a spark of cheer,
Moments that we hold so dear,
With zest in hearts and smiles so wide,
Together we feel that vibrant ride.

So gather 'round, let's celebrate,
The silly things that make us great,
With every bite and every cheer,
The essence of sweetness is always near.

Tangy Tales of Morning Glow

Mornings dance with zestful flair,
A wink, a smile, a citrus air.
Juggling woes like fruits so bright,
Tickled pink, we chase the light.

Chasing giggles down the lane,
Sour faces meet sweet rain.
With every twist, a joke unfolds,
A juicy tale that never grows old.

Pour some sunshine in your tea,
Life's a tart, but oh so free!
With a splash and a zestful cheer,
Let's make memories year by year.

Sunshine Spritz and Sour Notes

Under skies of cerulean hue,
We squeeze the day, it's good as new.
Twirling words like candy canes,
Tickled hearts, forget the chains.

Toasting to the quirky jest,
Wrap the sour in a fest.
Lemonade dreams in summer's light,
Mixing giggles, oh what a sight!

From citrus quests in offbeat rhyme,
Embracing sweetness, every time.
A pinch of joy, a dash of cheer,
With every sip, we hold it dear.

Lively Echoes of the Orchard

In orchards where the blossoms sway,
Fruity fun leads hearts astray.
Watch the critters dance and play,
Chasing drizzles through the fray.

An orchard's whisper, full of cheer,
Sour tunes that disappear.
Peeling laughter from unseen trees,
Harvest moments in the breeze.

Every fruit a story tells,
With giggles wrapped in citrus spells.
We gather 'round for hearty cheer,
In every bite, the joy is clear.

Sweet Relief in Tangy Times

When the world feels like a squeeze,
Look ahead, it's sure to please.
Wit and whimsy in every bite,
Sprinkling joy, a pure delight.

Sour notes that keep us bold,
Laughter's warming as days unfold.
We'll rendezvous with silly pranks,
In zestful pools of sunny thanks.

Fruits of mirth hang on each vine,
As we sip that sparkling brine.
In tangy times, let spirits soar,
With every chuckle, there's more in store.

The Bright Side of Bittersweet

When sour meets the sweet and bright,
A grin emerges with pure delight.
We toss our worries high in the air,
And catch each giggle, free of despair.

With every twist and every turn,
The wind whispers secrets we learn.
A sprinkle of zest, a dash of cheer,
Embrace the wacky, hold it dear.

Dancing in Citrus Groves

In groves where fruit bounces and sways,
We spin in circles, lost in a daze.
The sun beams down, a cheeky grin,
As we tangle our toes in sugary skin.

The branches sway like swing sets high,
We laugh and tumble, letting out a sigh.
Amongst the citrus, we break the mold,
Finding joy in stories untold.

Optimism from the Orchard

The trees stand tall, with arms open wide,
Inviting each creature for a joyous ride.
We pluck sweet memories, one by one,
As the orchard hums a tune of fun.

With every bite, a burst of glee,
A hint of mischief in every spree.
Chasing shadows and spinning round,
In the heart of nature, happiness is found.

Vibrant Days

Morning sun spills with bold designs,
Creating laughter in sun-drenched lines.
We trip on joy, in bright parade,
A wacky festival's serenade.

Every moment, a chance to play,
Grinning, skimming through the fray.
Bright blooms and giggles fill the air,
Painting our world, free from care.

Tangy Nights

As twilight drapes its playful gown,
The stars wink sweetly, wearing a crown.
We gather under a celestial spread,
With chuckles echoing, joy's widespread.

The moon's a slice of creamy pie,
We toast our dreams, letting laughter fly.
With zesty whispers in the warm breeze,
We find delight with carefree ease.

Sunny Days and Bitter Sips

Under the sun, we chase our dreams,
With icy drinks, we plot our schemes.
A twist of fate, a splash of cheer,
In this wild game, we've nothing to fear.

Sour notes dance with each bright laugh,
Juicy tales fill our crazy path.
With every sip, a story grows,
Mixing sweet giggles, the fun just flows.

Chasing shadows, we're on the run,
Brightened hearts share warmth like the sun.
Fruits of our labor in smiles we find,
Sipping on joy, leaving woes behind.

At sunset's call, let's raise a toast,
To moments we cherish and brag the most.
With every drop of fizzy delight,
Tomorrow we'll greet, who knows what's in sight!

The Citrus Serenade

In orchards bright, we roam and play,
Singing songs of a zesty day.
Peels fly high, the laughter spills,
As we dance among the rolling hills.

With every zest of citrus bright,
A sprinkle of joy, putting up a fight.
Sour grins turn to sweet refrains,
In this fruity jive, we have none to feign.

Tartness tickles, our spirits fly,
Chasing flutters that never die.
Grapefruits giggle in the midday sun,
While lemonade dreams begin to run.

From sunny skies, our hearts will sing,
Bitter beats make the laughter cling.
In every squeeze, new stories pour,
Together we thrive, forevermore!

Joyful Breezes and Sour Kisses

The winds whisper tales in bright hues,
While tangy surprises await our views.
Sour remarks shared with a grin,
Life's little pranks always begin.

A burst of brightness in cloudy schemes,
We savor the moments like sweetened creams.
With every gust, let laughter soar,
Finding joy where we once swore.

Dance in the zest of a playful breeze,
Bouncing around like buzzing bees.
A kiss of tang, a hearty laugh,
The sour moments, they make us half.

With playful jibes and cheeky roars,
We embrace the charms our heart adores.
In the mix of highs and lows we find,
A sweet embrace of the wittiest kind!

Zest for the Everyday

Awake to the buzz of morning's glow,
With cheerful quirks in tow we go.
Sour rhythms keep our day bright,
A hint of mischief in every bite.

Mornings rich with fruity delight,
Chasing shadows well into the night.
Jokes and jests like lemonade sips,
Pouring joy with our friendship drips.

Each day's a canvas, we paint it bold,
With shades of laughter, tales unfold.
Twisting fates and silly finds,
Create a zest that never winds.

So let's embrace the winks and grins,
For in every challenge, the fun begins.
A sprinkle of humor, a dash of cheer,
We'll savor this journey, year after year!

The Citrus Chronicles of Cheer

In a grove where giggles grow,
Lemons dance, putting on a show.
Sunshine drips from each bright slice,
Sour faces turn to giggly spice.

A jester's hat upon a tree,
Waving branches, wild and free.
Zesty jokes hop on the breeze,
Tickling noses with such ease.

Bumblebees buzz in joyful cheer,
Jetting off with fruit to spear.
Citrus pies with silly names,
Bringing forth delicious games.

We gather round to laugh and squeeze,
Spicy punch, and tickled knees.
Throwing zest in every plate,
In this grove, we celebrate.

Sparkling Moments in Orchard Shadows

Underneath the leafy shade,
Fruits of laughter are displayed.
Orchards buzz with jolly tunes,
As sunlight spins around like loons.

A sprinkle here, a chuckle there,
Citrus mischief fills the air.
Foot-stomping, flat-out goofy fun,
With each bright orb, we slice and run.

Pies and pranks, a playful mix,
Tangy tarts and jelly kicks.
Every bite's a burst of cheer,
Sweetened with a wink and sneer.

In the shadows, tales unfold,
Squirrels whisper secrets bold.
A sparkling day, a zany crew,
Orchard magic, bright and true.

Squeeze the Day

Rise and shine, the sun's ablaze,
Time to have some silly plays.
With a twist and mighty pump,
Come on, let's create a thump!

Zesty smiles on every face,
Yummy drinks, it's time we race.
Pouring joy in every glass,
With a splash, we make it pass.

Chasing sunsets with a grin,
Bouncing 'round like mad, we spin.
Juicy dreams, so sweetly spun,
Squeeze the day, let's have some fun!

In this bright and citrus world,
Every flag of joy unfurled.
We lift our cups to skies so blue,
Together, tangled, me and you.

Sunlight on Citrus Skins

Beneath the rays, we frolic wide,
With zesty giggles, nothing to hide.
Sunshine tickles every bit,
As we dance and never quit.

Pale yellow globes hang from the vine,
Each a treasure, sweet, divine.
We juggle dreams, and lemons too,
Splashing colors, bright and new.

Silly faces all around,
Every burst, a joyful sound.
Lemonade cascades like a stream,
Chasing after every gleam.

In the glow of golden hour,
We find our muse, we find our power.
With citrus kisses on our skin,
Laughter flows, where joy begins.

Joy in Every Zest

When things get sour, don't frown,
Just grab a slice, turn that around.
Add a sprinkle of cheer, a pinch of zest,
In the silly dance, we find our best.

A tiny grin, a hearty laugh,
Beats all the gloom, it's a magic craft.
With every chuckle, the clouds are thin,
So let the giggles and good vibes spin!

We'll twist and turn, in a merry way,
Citrus smiles make the gray decay.
With each bright burst, happiness flies,
And lemony joys light up the skies!

So next time life gives you a twist,
Just take a leap—it's too good to miss.
Bitter or sweet, it's all a jest,
In the carnival of joy, we're truly blessed.

Tangy Moments

In the backyard sun, we chase our dreams,
Where giggles echo and laughter beams.
With every prank, a story unfolds,
Tales of the silly, brave, and bold.

An impromptu splash, a lemon fight,
Squeals of joy in the fading light.
We paint the world in colors bright,
With laughter that sparkles like stars at night.

When life gets tricky, take a break,
Dance on the grass, for fun's own sake.
Jump through puddles, sing out loud,
In each moment, let joy be found!

Collect the quirks like a prized bouquet,
Share them around and brighten the day.
For every giggle adds to the cheer,
In this wild, wacky, whimsical sphere!

Sweetness in Sours

Sipping on drink with a twist of fun,
Mixing up joy under the shining sun.
A playful heart, and a snappy grin,
Who knew sour could lead to a win?

Pass the fun, let's mix and twirl,
Watch the smiles in a happy whirl.
With silly faces and splashes wide,
We toast to the moments, together, side by side.

A giggle here, a chuckle there,
With every laugh, we lighten the air.
Sweet surprise in every little fool,
Life's a party, let's keep it cool!

So shake off worries like dust from shoes,
Join the frolic, we can't refuse.
In the sour lies sweetness, we can bet,
With each merry moment, we won't forget.

The Bright Side of Bitter

When things get tough, just take a pause,
Look for the bright through life's little flaws.
With a wink and a grin, you'll soon find,
That humor can chase the worries behind.

A sour moment? It's just a game,
Add some zest, and you'll feel no shame.
With each tight squeeze, let giggles grow,
In every frown, there's a secret glow!

So pitch a fit or throw a play,
Silly antics clear the gray away.
Dance through the chaos, laugh out loud,
In the bittersweet stories, we're forever proud!

For every twist adds to our tale,
With bubbly humor, we cannot fail.
So here's to the mess and the laughter inside,
In this wild ride, let's enjoy the slide!

Bright Chords of Existence

In a world where smiles collide,
Jokes tumble like rolling tide.
We gather round with hope held high,
And let our worries slip and fly.

With silly hats and grand charades,
We weave our dreams in playful shades.
Each chuckle burst—a spark of light,
As we embrace the joyful night.

Dancing shadows on the wall,
Echoing laughter, a carnival.
Tickles and giggles fill the air,
In this festival of goofy flair.

As bright chords of our hearts align,
We sip on drinks both sweet and fine.
Every moment, a gleeful tease,
We savor joy, our happy disease.

Fragrant Whispers of Joy

In fields where wild whispers roam,
We chase the sun, we call it home.
Petals dance on breezy trails,
While giggles ride on crafty gales.

The scent of mischief fills the air,
As friends unite without a care.
With jokes so fresh, like citrus pie,
We toast to moments passing by.

A splash of fun in every bite,
Our hearts alight like stars at night.
With playful grins that bloom and shine,
We celebrate, each sip divine.

In fragrant whispers, dreams take flight,
In silly stories, pure delight.
Together laughing, come what may,
In every moment, joy will stay.

Playful Breezes Through the Orchard

Amidst the trees where shadows play,
We frolic free from blunders gray.
With fruity jests, we skip and sway,
In sunshine's warmth, we seize the day.

Breezes chatter, tales unfold,
With every giggle, laughter bold.
We toss our worries in the air,
And let the zest of fun declare.

Our footsteps dance on grass so green,
In orchard realms, where joys convene.
We swing on branches, hearts ablaze,
In charming games, we spin and craze.

With playful breezes swirling 'round,
Our merry hearts unite, unbound.
Through laughter's echo, sweet and clear,
We sip on sunshine, year by year.

The Citrus Dance

Beneath the sun's warm, golden glance,
We twirl around in vibrant stance.
With zest and zeal, our spirits prance,
In joyful tunes, we start the dance.

Bright orbs of cheer hang from the trees,
We gather 'neath the subtle breeze.
With each sweet bite, a burst of fun,
Our revelry has just begun.

Chasing shadows, spinning fast,
We laugh and cheer, our worries cast.
In every tangle, giggles rise,
As citrus dreams fill up the skies.

The citrus dance—a mirrored delight,
Connecting souls in playful flight.
Through sunshine's kiss, we find our chance,
To celebrate with glee, we dance.

Zesty Journeys Through the Seasons

In springtime's glimmer, we dance in delight,
With laughter like bubbles, we're feeling just right.
Golden days sparkle, like sunshine in play,
We'll chase clouds of joy, come what may.

Summer comes blazing, with a cheeky sun grin,
We splash through the puddles, let the fun begin.
Chasing till sunset, with ice cream in hand,
Our giggles resound like a playful band.

As autumn whispers, the leaves start to twirl,
We toss them like confetti, let our hearts whirl.
In cozy sweaters, we sip cider's cheer,
Each moment a treasure, our hearts feeling near.

Winter snuggles softly, with snowflakes that tease,
We build frosty castles, with giggles and case.
Hot cocoa hugs us, to melt all the chill,
Together we twinkle, and time seems to still.

Radiance in Every Drop

A drizzle of sunshine, through each morning dew,
With twinkling droplets, the world feels brand new.
We dance in the rain, with our boots on so bright,
Each slosh and each splash is pure joyous delight.

From puddles we leap, with squeals that resound,
As raindrops become music, a crackling sound.
We giggle at storms, as they rumble and roll,
For every thick cloud, there's a bright silver scroll.

As sunbeams do shimmer through each raindrop's grace,
We treasure the moments, in this merry race.
With wet hair a-tousled, those wild, wavy curls,
We twirl and we spin, like carefree little girls.

In nature's bright laughter, we find our sweet song,
Through every odd weather, we'll always belong.
Each storm is but laughter, each ray a warm hug,
With radiant memories, let our hearts snug.

Cheerful Blossoms and Tangy Trails

In fields of bright blossoms, where colors collide,
We skip past the daisies, with giggles to glide.
Petals drift lightly, in fragrant arrays,
With every new journey, new mischief displays.

Through tangy green pathways, with friends side by side,
We munch on sweet morsels, and take joy in the ride.
With butterflies dancing, and breezes that tease,
We share endless stories beneath shady trees.

The sun casts a glow on our whimsical way,
With echoes of laughter that linger and sway.
We splash in the streams, like playful young sprites,
With heartbeats of joy chasing colorful sights.

As dusk starts to fall, with stars in the air,
We dream of tomorrow, with spirits laid bare.
In every adventure, we find a bright spark,
With cheerful reminders, we'll light up the dark.

Embracing the Sweetness of Today

The clock gently ticks, as the magic unfolds,
With moments so sweet, in each story retold.
We take time to savor, the small things that glow,
With smiles that connect us, like rivers that flow.

In laughter we gather, like bees to the bloom,
Spinning tales over cookies, igniting the room.
With friends all around us, the warmth multiplies,
As joy fills the air, like stars in the skies.

We dive into now, with open hearts wide,
With friendship like sunshine, our worries subside.
In every quick moment, we find pure delight,
Transforming the ordinary into something bright.

So here's to the echoes of laughter and fun,
To cherish the sweetness when day is all done.
With each little hug, and the smiles we relay,
We'll treasure this journey, embracing today.

The Citrus Carousel

Round and round the zest does spin,
With giggles trapped like fruit within.
Pies tossed up in the summer air,
A slice of joy, a citrus flare.

Bouncing balls of bright delight,
Chuckles dance with every bite.
Sour moods take a joyful swim,
In lemonade, the world's akin.

Curly straws and fruity tricks,
Sprinkled smiles, the perfect mix.
When the world is feeling gruff,
A citrus twist can be enough.

So take your seat, the ride is free,
In this roundabout, let's just be.
Fresh laughter fills the sunny sky,
On this carousel, we'll fly high.

Flavorful Happiness Lab

In a lab where giggles brew,
Gummy bears and soda too.
Flavors burst and dance around,
In bubbling pots, joy is found.

Dashing sprinkles, crazy fun,
Cooking smiles under the sun.
Pops of color, tasting dreams,
In this lab, the laughter beams.

Mixing secrets, sweet and tart,
Each concoction is a work of art.
With playful swirls and wild glee,
Creating happiness, come see!

So grab a spoon and dig right in,
Flavored giggles, where we win.
In every bite, a little cheer,
In this lab, we have no fear.

Whispers of Playfulness

In the garden, shadows prance,
Flowers giggle, bugs do a dance.
Whispers float on breezy tunes,
Bouncing laugh like playful balloons.

Sunshine sprinkles on the ground,
Each soft chuckle, joy is found.
Petals stir with cheeky grace,
Swaying lightly, just like lace.

Rippling streams of giggly bliss,
Every drop a playful kiss.
Nature's voice, a joyful hum,
In its laughter, we succumb.

So join the dance, let worries cease,
In whispered giggles, find your peace.
With every step, a lighter heart,
In the meadow, we're all art.

The Ripple of Gleefulness

Toss a pebble in the pond,
Watch the ripples swirl and bond.
Each laugh creates a little wave,
In water's embrace, hilarity's brave.

Jumping splashes, bright delight,
Giggles chase the fading light.
As the sun sinks low and fast,
We savor moments meant to last.

Little cheers bounce off the shore,
In every giggle, we explore.
The glimmering waves, a play parade,
In this playground, joy is made.

So, let's splash in pools of cheer,
With every giggle, joy draws near.
In the ripples, laughter flows,
A world of joy, where happiness grows.

Savoring the Sweets Amidst the Zest

In a world of bright and bold,
We find the joys that stories told.
With tangy smiles and sugary goods,
We traverse the paths of our lively woods.

A splash of humor, a dash of cream,
In every mishap, we twist and beam.
With every sip, a giggle greets,
The sour turns sweet in our tasty feats.

Laughing under citrus trees,
Sunshine whispers in the breeze.
With every twist, we make a mess,
It's part of charm, no need to stress.

So raise a glass to joy's delight,
In zest and cheer, we take flight.
For every twist of fate we find,
A sumptuous grin is well-designed.

Hues of Joy and the Taste of Grit

In shades of yellow, bright and clear,
We dance with moments, full of cheer.
With every sip of citrus zest,
We savor dreams, we are truly blessed.

A pinch of humor, a splash of fun,
Life's greatest tasks are best done.
The journey's trials, we fondly greet,
With laughter echoing on the street.

When troubles come in shades of grey,
We sprinkle joy and sway away.
Finding the strength in every sip,
With giggles shared from laugh to lip.

In every sip, a brave new start,
Embracing every quirk, we play our part.
For with good friends and warmth to give,
In colors bright, we truly live.

Cheerful Whispers from the Tree

Underneath the branches wide,
We gather round in joy and pride.
With whispers sweet and stories grand,
We share our secrets, hand in hand.

The playful breeze brings giggles near,
From every fruit, the joy is clear.
The world spins merry, nothing to fear,
With every grin, the path is dear.

Bright fruits of humor spring to life,
In this mirthful joyous strife.
We toss our cares to skies above,
We toast to sunshine, laugh, and love.

So gather 'round, let voices soar,
In every chuckle, we want more.
With unified hearts, take a chance,
In light and laughter, we all dance.

Sunlit Mirth and Harvest's Bounty

When golden rays begin to shine,
We cook up plans, a grand design.
With baskets filled, our spirits lift,
We gather 'round, a treasured gift.

Through gardens rich with laughter's song,
In every footstep, we can't go wrong.
With every laugh, we paint the air,
As we partake in joy laid bare.

The kitchen bustling, pots in play,
With zestful twists, we find our way.
Even if the recipe strays,
There's charm in silliness that stays.

So here's to moments, sweet and bright,
In every mischief, pure delight.
With every bite, our hearts embrace,
In sun-kissed glee, we find our place.

Serendipity in a Glass

With a twist of fate, I take a sip,
Sugar and zest upon my lip.
Bubbles rise like giggles, so sweet,
Quenching thirst, oh what a treat!

Sunshine dances in my drink,
As I ponder, laugh, and wink.
A splash of joy, a dash of cheer,
Sipping happiness, crystal clear.

Don't you dare forget your straw,
It might just be the perfect flaw!
Sip slowly, enjoy the swirl,
In this glass, a funny world.

Cheers to moments, bubbling bright,
Finding joy in silly plights.
Fizzy dreams and merry talks,
With each sip, my laughter walks.

Cheery Notes in My Melody

Sing a tune, let laughter fly,
Jokes and jests like clouds in the sky.
Play your heart on strings of cheer,
With every note, I've no more fear.

Rhythms dance in playful spree,
A comic twist, just you and me.
Humming softly, chuckles grow,
In this song, our spirits flow.

Harmony spills like spilled hot tea,
Silly rhymes set our minds free.
So strum your joy, let voices blend,
In this melody, we'll never end.

Chords of glee, let's laugh and shout,
In this tune, we'll twist about.
Every laugh, a note we play,
Creating joy in our own way.

Prickles and Pearls

In a garden filled with strange delight,
Prickly weeds and pearls so bright.
Giggles sprout among the thorns,
Tickled pink in rosy morns.

Finding treasures in the rough,
Laughter grows, it's just enough.
With every poke of nature's sting,
Joy emerges like spring's first fling.

Oh the jesters that plants can be,
Dancing rhymes so effortlessly.
Through prickles come laughter's grace,
In this patch, we find our place.

Wandering paths of joy and jest,
Chasing smiles, we feel our best.
Here amidst the tangled blooms,
Laughter fills the vibrant rooms.

Vibrant Visions of Tomorrow

With colors bright, we sketch and play,
Dreams unfold in a silly way.
Dancing brushes, paint the sky,
Let's create what makes hearts fly.

Each stroke a giggle, each splash a grin,
Imagining the fun we'll win.
In a world where jesters roam,
We'll paint our hearts a cheerful home.

Tomorrow's canvas, wide and free,
With silly symbols, come laugh with me.
We'll weave our stories, vivid and bold,
In every hue, the joy unfolds.

So mix the colors, let's start anew,
In this vibrant scene, just me and you.
With laughter as our guiding light,
We'll paint the world, oh what a sight!

A Taste of Vigor

In the morning sun, I wake up bright,
With a grin so wide, it feels just right.
A splash of zest in my cup so bold,
Today's adventures are waiting to unfold.

The world is ripe with giggles and cheer,
As I jive along, I forget my fear.
With every step, a bounce in my shoes,
I dance through moments, I simply can't lose.

Juicy Exuberance

A citrus twist ignites my soul,
Silliness sprinkles, and I feel whole.
Each chuckle fresh, like a morning dew,
Filling the air with flavors anew.

Under the sun, I twirl and play,
Making shadows that laugh, come what may.
With every giggle, the day does shine,
In this bouncy world, I sip and dine.

Bubbles of Glee

Pop! fizz! a sparkle in the air,
Giggles bubble like soda flare.
Each drip and drop holds a joke inside,
With whimsy and joy I cannot hide.

I whirl around like a playful breeze,
Twirling laughter, bending knees.
With fizzy laughter, the world shines bright,
Every moment's a feast, delight in sight!

Colorful Sprays of Ambition

Bright splashes color my every goal,
Chasing dreams that ignite my soul.
With hues of joy, I'm ready to fight,
Spinning through days that feel just right.

With a wink and smile, I take my aim,
The sky's the limit, it's all a game.
Each colorful dream, a joy to chase,
In the chase of fun, I find my place.

Tangled Threads of Cheer

In the garden of giggles, we dance and we sway,
Juggling bright dreams, in a whimsical play.
With mischief and joy, we spin tales unbound,
Every stumble's a laugh, where delight can be found.

Chasing the shadows that tickle the sun,
We wear silly hats, oh what reckless fun!
In a world full of quirks, we embrace every blip,
Pouring sugar on troubles, let happiness sip.

We barter our woes for a slapstick surprise,
Finding joy in the chaos, oh how time flies!
With a wink and a nod, we create our own fate,
Laughter's the thread that we use to create.

So gather your friends, and let folly ignite,
With giggles and joy, we'll carry the night.
In our tapestry woven with glee and good cheer,
Every silly moment is what we hold dear.

Twists of Fate and Flavor

A twist of a lime in the punch bowl's delight,
Turns the mundane into a colorful bite.
With laughter like bubbles that fizz in the air,
We sip on our dreams, without a single care.

A dash of the wild and a sprinkle of glee,
We cook up the moments, just you wait and see.
Mixing up flavors, we dance on the ground,
Every taste a surprise, with joy we are bound.

When fortune throws curves, we chuckle and smile,
For the sweetness in chaos is truly worthwhile.
In this feast of existence, we feast on the wry,
With each twist and turn, we're reaching for the sky.

So grab a fork, dear friend, it's a ride just begun,
In the kitchen of fate, we stir up the fun.
Let's savor the moments, the strange and the rare,
For laughter's the seasoning, we'll happily share.

Nature's Kaleidoscope

In the meadow of colors, we spin round and round,
Every petal a giggle, where happiness is found.
With butterflies winking, and daisies that cheer,
Nature holds secrets that bring joy near.

The trees tell of stories that dance in the breeze,
Whispers of humor that tickle with ease.
Raindrops like laughter sprinkle down from the sky,
Gathering glimmers of glee as they fly.

Like a painter's palette, the world's a delight,
Swirls of sheer madness abound in plain sight.
Each moment a twinkle, a sparkle, a wink,
In this colored carnival, we pause and we think.

So chase after rainbows, let whimsy unfold,
In the canvas of nature, there's magic untold.
We'll dance through the colors, in harmony play,
For joy's in the journey, come what may.

Radiance in Simplicity

In the quiet of morning, a giggle escapes,
From the warmth of the sun and the playful drapes.
Every smile a beacon, brightening the day,
In simple exchanges, we lose our dismay.

With bubbles of banter that float through the air,
The joy of connection, incredibly rare.
In the stillness of moments, hilarity swells,
As we gather our laughter like shimmering shells.

Each chuckle a treasure, each grin a delight,
We clad ourselves proudly in joy's soft invite.
The mundane transforms with each tickle and tease,
In the glow of good fun, we find our sweet ease.

So let's treasure the little, the silly, the small,
For in radiant moments, we live after all.
In the arms of simplicity, we'll joyfully sway,
Creating a symphony, come what may.

www.ingramcontent.com/pod-product-compliance
Lightning Source LLC
Chambersburg PA
CBHW051631160426
43209CB00004B/598